MUTTS

by PATRICK McDonnell

Andrews and McMeel
A Universal Press Syndicate Company
Kansas City

Mutts is distributed internationally by King Features Syndicate, Inc. For information write King Features Syndicate, Inc., 216 East 45th Street, New York, New York 10017.

ISBN: 0-8362-1025-5

Library of Congress Catalog Card Number: 95-80761

98 99 00 01 WOR 10 9 8 7 6

Foreword

What's the highest compliment I can pay Patrick McDonnell? He keeps coming up with ideas I wish I had thought of myself. A perfect example would be the strip where Earl and Mooch, the cat, are looking at a flock of birds and Mooch says, "Hey, I know that guy."

To me, *Mutts* is exactly what a comic strip should be. It is always fun to look at, and the two main characters are wonderfully innocent. Patrick has created a little world that exists within itself. Everyone in *Mutts*, from the little pet fish to the butcher behind his counter, is funny. Earl, of course, holds it all together and as always it is the way he is drawn that makes him so good. It's hard to believe that after 100 years of comics, Patrick could come up with a new and perfect little dog. I like everything about *Mutts*.

Charles M. Schulz

Charles M. Schulz,
Creator of *Peanuts*

TO MY WIFE, FAMILY, FRIENDS,
AND DOG.

EARL STOPS FROZEN IN HIS TRACKS.

WHICH WILL HE ANSWER? THE CALL OF THE WILD...

OR THE CALL OF THE CAN OPENER?

WR-R-R-R-R.

YOU START AT THE BOTTOM...

BUT EVENTUALLY...

MAKE IT TO THE TOP.

IT'S THE SUREST WAY TO GET A HEAD.

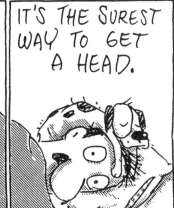

EARL WATCHES THE WORLD GO BY.

YES, SIR.

NO DIFFERENT SIDEWAYS.

McDonnell.

8

DOG THERMOMETER:

70°   80°   90°   100°

CAT THERMOMETER:

16

17

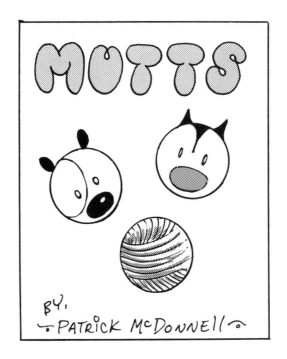

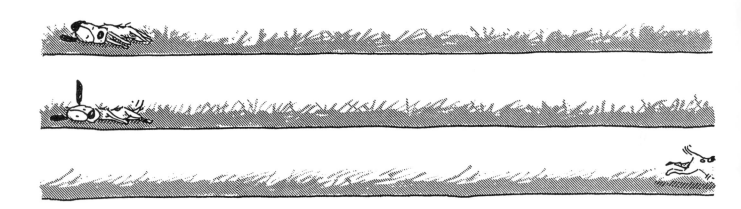

ARF ARF

RUFF RUFF RUFF

THAT'S ODD...

I FORGOT WHAT I WAS BARKING ABOUT.

FLOWERS.

FORGET·ME·NOTS.

SOME SAY HE'S "ALWAYS LOOKING FOR TROUBLE".

SOME CALL HIM "NOSY"

WE LEAN TOWARD HE HAS A "LUST FOR LIFE."

McDONNELL.

I WONDER WHAT I MUST LOOK LIKE TO YOU...

MY COUSIN SHAMU.

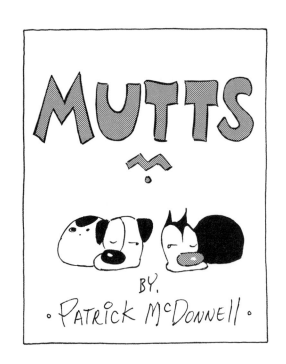

HEY, I'M GOING TO TAKE A "CATNAP."

OH NO YOU'RE NOT! YOU CAN'T—DOGS CAN'T TAKE A CATNAP!!!

OOOH GEE— LOOK AT ME— A WITTLE SWEEPY PUTTY TAT...

YOU CAN'T! YOU CAN'T!

OKAY, OKAY...

PUR·R·R·R·R

GRRR.

GRRR.

POW

31

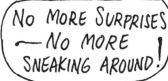

HERE, MOOCH, A LITTLE BELL FOR YOUR COLLAR SO EVERYONE CAN HEAR YOU COMING...

NO MORE SURPRISES — NO MORE SNEAKING AROUND!

HONEY.... I DID BUY TWO! HA! HA!

YES, DEAR, WE CAN PUT THAT ONE ON MY WALLET!

Tinkle Tinkle

WHAT'S THAT?

TINKLE TINKLE

THE LADY I LIVE WITH PUT A WARNING BELL ON ME! WHAT!? DO I LOOK DANGEROUS!?!

HEY, LOOK OUT EVERYBODY, TINKLE TINKLE HERE COMES THE "KRAZED KILLER KITTY KAT"... RUN FOR YOUR SORRY LIVES!!!

SMART LADY

LOCK YOUR DOORS AND WINDOWS!!!

MOOCH HAS BEEN BRANDED WITH A BELL... TINKLE TINKLE

AARGH
TINKLE TINKLE

UMPH
TINKLE TINKLE

AII·E·E·E
TINKLE TINKLE
TINKLE TINKLE

IT'S A GOOD THING I HAVE NINE LIVES — 'CAUSE THIS ONE IS OVER.

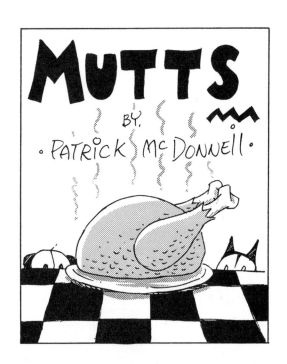

YIPEE!
AN OLD SOCK!

IT SMELLED OLD.

MY HOUSE.   MY BED.   MY SPOT.   MY LIFE.

HEY, EARL, WHAT ARE YOU DOING UP THERE FOR SO LONG?

WAITING.

HA! YOU DOGS AND YOUR STUBBORN LOYALTY. WHAT ARE YOU WAITING FOR?

OZZIE WENT HOLIDAY FOOD SHOPPING.

DO YOU THINK HE'LL GET THOSE LITTLE PARTY SARDINES?

HEY, WHAT ARE YOU DOING HERE ANYWAY?

I'M WAITING FOR FOOD. LIKE YOU.

No. I MEAN HOW COME YOU'RE NOT AT YOUR HOUSE?

OH

IT'S A CRAZY SCENE OVER THERE—I HAD TO GET OUT.... SOMEONE TRIED TO CLIMB THE CHRISTMAS TREE AND LIKE AN IDIOT KNOCKED IT OVER!

WHAT A MESS

How DID YOU DO THAT?

WHY DOES EVERYONE THINK IT'S ME!?!

HEY, LOOK OVER THERE! GOING DOOR TO DOOR WITH HIS BIG POUCH FILLED WITH GOODIES...

WHERE?

THERE! THERE'S SANDY CLAWS!

WHO HIM!?!

OVER HERE, SAINT NIX! IT'S ME!

THAT'S THE GUY WHO DELIVERS OUR MAIL, YOU NUT.

SURE... LIKE SANTA HAS TIME FOR THAT!

PATRICK McDONNELL

ZIP

MUTTS

BY,
PATRICK. Mc Donnell

IT WAS ONE OF THOSE WINTER STORMS

WHERE YOU LOSE YOUR BEARINGS. WHERE YOU LOSE YOURSELF.

YOU TRY TO FOCUS ON SOMETHING. ANYTHING.

NOTHING. THEN YOU HOWL — A CALL OF THE WILD TO SOMEONE. ANY ONE.

NO ONE. AND THEN YOU HOWL JUST TO CURSE THE DARKNESS.

ONLY TO HEAR BACK THE HOWL OF A COLD, HEARTLESS WIND.

DO YOU WANT TO COME BACK IN ALREADY?

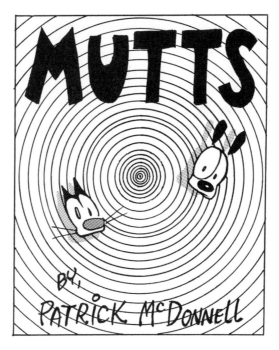

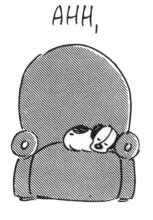

AHH,

TO GET LOST

IN THE BIG CHAIR.

MUTTS
by.

IT TOOK MONTHS! IT TOOK YEARS!!! BUT I FINALLY **KILLED** ALL THE WEEDS! KILLED ALL THE FUNGUS, AND DANDELIONS, TOO! **KILLED** ALL THE BUGS! KILLED ALL THE GRUBS! GOT **RID** OF THE SHADE TREES, THE MOLES AND THE SQUIRRELS! AND, OH YES, THE BIRDS AND THE DEER! **ALL** FOR THIS— THE SPECTACLE OF MY PICTURE PERFECT, IMMACULATE GREEN LAWN!

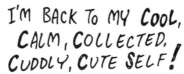

80

A PIECE OF PROVOLONE CHEESE (THE "GOOD" STUFF)— TO LURE OUT **THAT** MOUSE!

NO ONE CAN RESIST **THAT** SMELL!

GIMME DAT CHEESE!

IT'S **MINE!**

WE HAVE **NO** MORE CHEESE TO LURE OUT **THAT** MOUSE.

NO WORRY— I'LL DO MY "MOUSIE" DANCE.

MOUSIE!

SHMOUSIE!

MOUSIE!

DID ANYTHING COME **OUT?**

MY LUNCH CAME CLOSE.

C'MON...

PEEP.

I HADN'T HEARD A 'PEEP' OUT OF HIM ALL DAY.

86

94

95

MUTTS

by
PATRICK McDONNELL

IF YOU'RE GOING TO BE LOST, IT MIGHT AS WELL BE IN THE "MAGIC FOREST."

WHAT'S SO MAGICAL ABOUT THIS FOREST?

WELL, JUST **LOOK** AROUND YOU ... FRESH AIR, CLEAN WATER, HEALTHY TREES, ABUNDANT WILDLIFE, **NO** CARS, **NO** TOURISTS, **NO** SOUVENIR STANDS! **HECK**, NOWADAYS...

THAT'S GOT TO BE MAGIC.

COME AND VISIT ANYTIME! I'M NOT GOING ANYWHERE.

ANOTHER MALL COMING SOON

WHAT'S WITH **HIM**?

EARL MISSES HIS OZZIE

HA! BREAK YOUR BONDS OF DOMESTICITY! RETURN TO YOUR ROOTS! TOUCH THE EARTH! JUMP IN THE MUD! FEEL THE STIFLING HEAT! SWEAT! HUNT FOR FOOD! GET BITTEN BY BUGS! BE IN CONSTANT **FEAR** OF PREDATORS...

WOULD THIS "OZZIE" LIKE A CUTE WITTLE FROG?

MUTTS

by.

• PATRICK McDONNELL •

mutts

• by PATRICK McDONNELL •

THERE HE GOES AGAIN... YESH.

DARN, I WISH WE WERE ALLOWED TO CROSS THE STREET. YESH.

MOOCH, **WHAT** ARE YOU DOING UP THAT TREE?

I FIGURE TO **CATCH** A SQUIRREL - I MUST **THINK** LIKE A SQUIRREL.

BONK

GET DOWN HERE YOU YELLOW-BELLY COWARD!

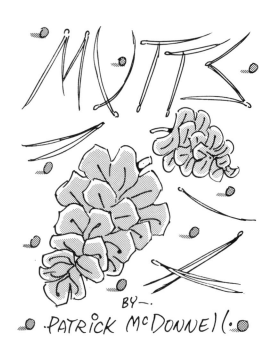

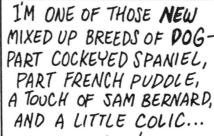

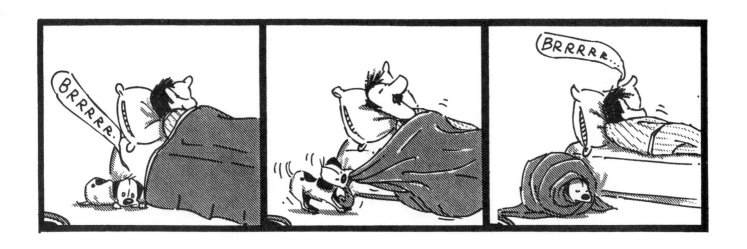